POINTLESS THINGS TO DO

ROBERT THOMPSON

WARNER BOOKS

D0273751

A *Warner* Book

First published in Great Britain in 1995

Copyright © Robert Thompson 1995

This edition published by Warner Books in 1995

The moral right of the author has been asserted.

The original **POINTLESS THINGS TO DO THIS WEEK** has appeared
in *The Spectator*.

A CIP catalogue record for this book is available from the British Library.

ISBN 0 7515 1091 2

Printed in and bound in Great Britain by
BPC Hazell Books Ltd, a Member of the British Printing Company Ltd

Warner Books
A Division of
Little, Brown and Company (UK)
Brettenham House
Lancaster Place
London WC2E 7EN

POINTLESS THINGS TO DO

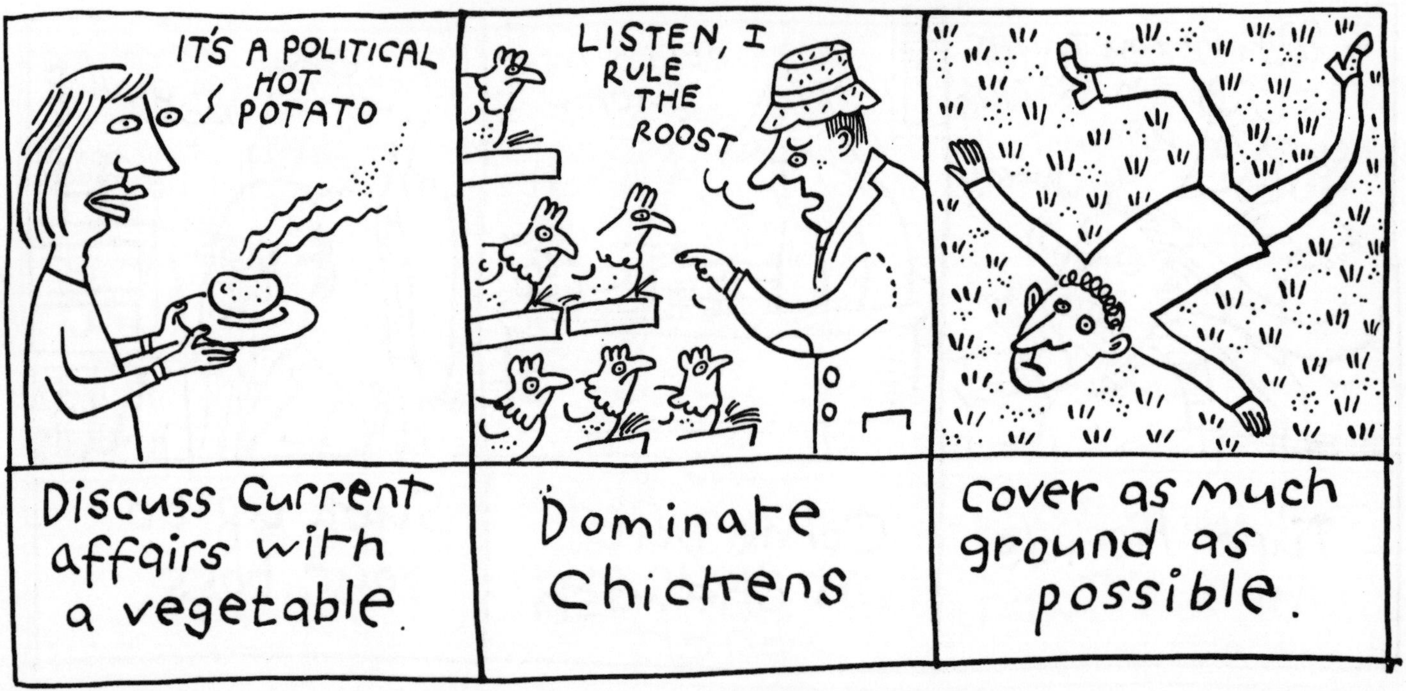

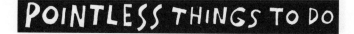

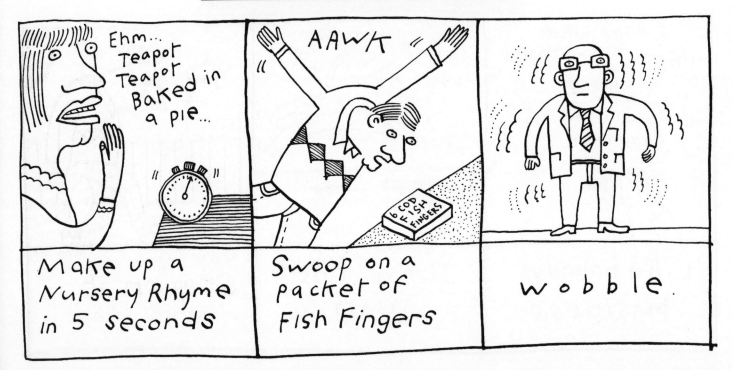

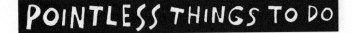

POINTLESS THINGS TO DO

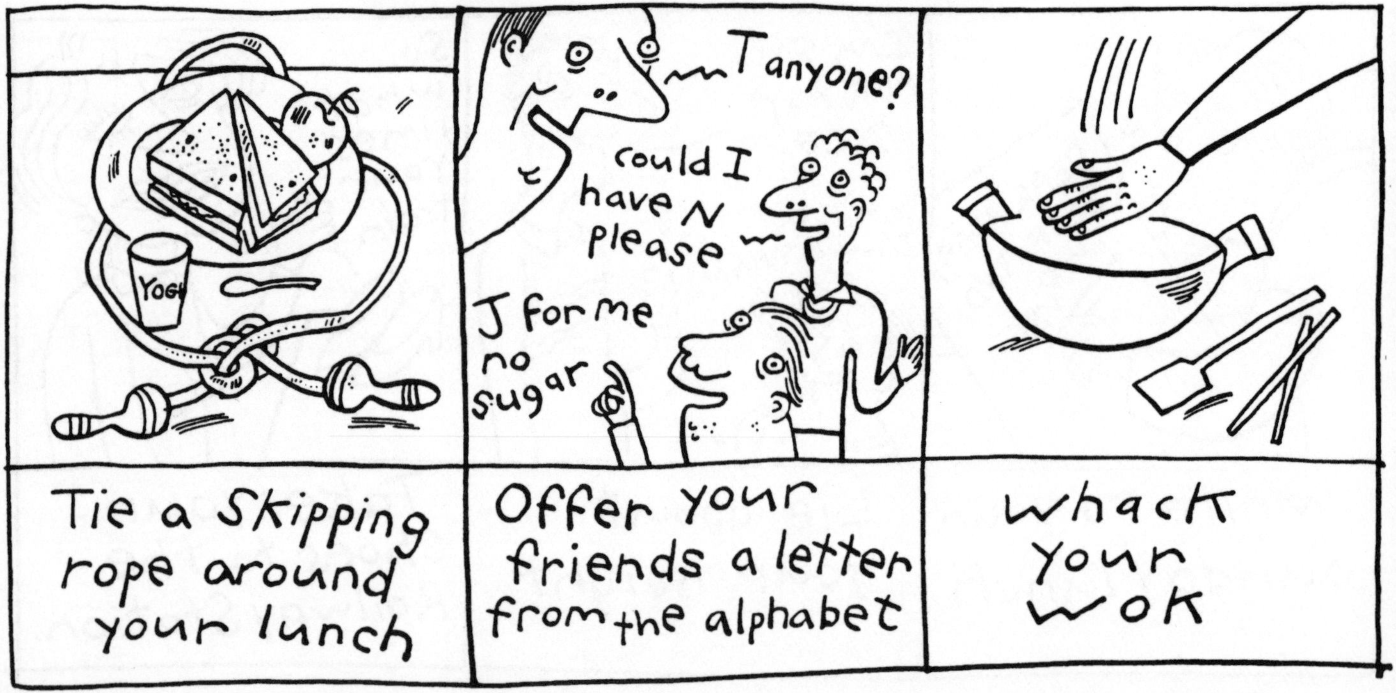

POINTLESS THINGS TO DO
HELLO, HOW'S YOUR BACTERIA?
Engage in small talk.
THERE IT IS!
See the World.
NOT IN MY BACK YARD
Throw away your dustbin.

POINTLESS THINGS TO DO

Put your watch backwards 5 hours and speak with an American accent.

Label everything.

Act like a clock all Wednesday.

POINTLESS THINGS TO DO

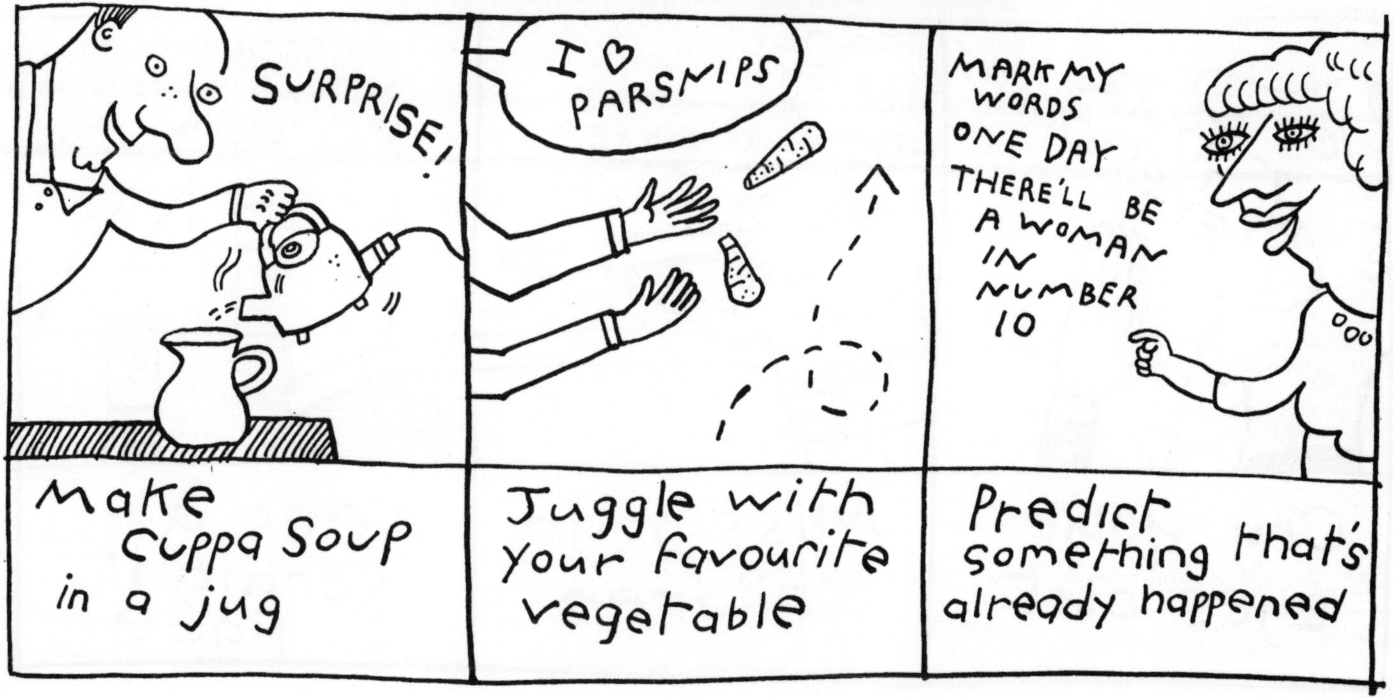

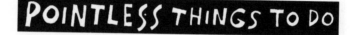

POINTLESS THINGS TO DO

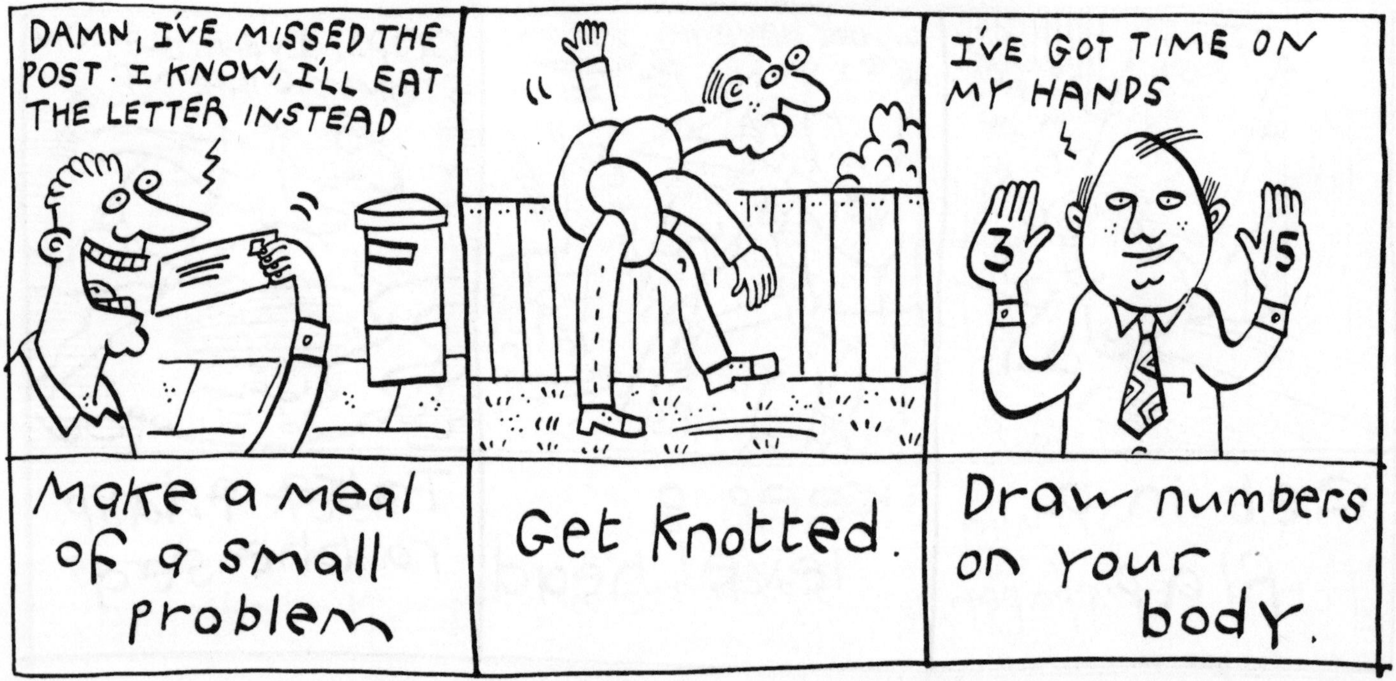

☐	CREATURE FEATURES	Dave Follows	£3.50
☐	THE FAR SIDE	Gary Larson	£4.99
☐	THE PRE-HISTORY OF THE FAR SIDE	Gary Larson	£9.99
☐	FAR SIDE GALLERY 4	Gary Larson	£8.99
☐	THE AUTHORITATIVE CALVIN & HOBBES	Bill Watterson	£8.99
☐	HOMICIDAL PSYCHO JUNGLE CAT	Bill Watterson	£7.99
☐	WILES ON THE WATER	Arnold Wiles	£7.99

This diverse range of cartoon collections published by Warner Books can be ordered from the following address:

Little, Brown and Company (UK)
P.O. Box 11
Falmouth
Cornwall TR10 9EN.

Alternatively you may fax your order to the above address.
Fax No. 01326 317444

Payments can be made as follows: cheque, postal order (payable to Little, Brown and Company) or by credit cards, Visa/Access. Do not send cash or currency. UK customers and BFPO please allow £1.00 for postage and packing for the first book, plus 50p for the second book, plus 30p for each additional book up to a maximum charge of £3.00 (7 books plus).

Overseas customers including Ireland please allow £2.00 for the first book, plus £1.00 for the second book, plus 50p for each additional book.

Name (BLOCK LETTERS) _____

Address _____

_____

_____

☐ I enclose my remittance for _____

☐ I wish to pay by Access/Visa Card

Number ☐☐☐☐☐☐☐☐☐☐☐☐☐☐☐

Card Expiry Date ☐☐☐☐